Manna
FOR THE
JOURNEY

Andrew L. Smith

WestBow
PRESS
A DIVISION OF THOMAS NELSON

WestBow Press books may be ordered through booksellers or by contacting:

WestBow Press
A Division of Thomas Nelson
1663 Liberty Drive
Bloomington, IN 47403
www.westbowpress.com
1-(866) 928-1240

ISBN: 978-1-4497-4561-5 (hc)
ISBN: 978-1-4497-4563-9 (sc)
ISBN: 978-1-4497-4562-2 (e)

Library of Congress Control Number: 2012906019

Printed in the United States of America

WestBow Press rev. date: 4/11/2012

PREFACE

God provided manna for the ancient Hebrews on their journey from Egypt to the Holy Land. The manna was adequate for only a day, except for Friday's manna, which lasted through the Sabbath. Likewise, we are given daily spiritual sustenance when we look for it. It comes in different ways. Much of my manna has come from the end of my pen.

For over fifty years, my pen and I have written on small scraps of paper, margins of books, journals, and anything else that happened to be available at the time. I've filed away thoughts, musings, opinions, and other emotions in the nooks and crannies I could find. Over time, I've revised, enlarged, reduced and otherwise modified some of them until they ended up as writings to be shared with friends. Some responded by saying my writings were interesting or that they had never looked at things that way before.

Most of the time these writings presents a perception a little off center, offering a different way of contemplating a thought or a verse. They are, in a way, reflections a little fractured and sometimes a little distorted. They provide a different way of seeing life. I hope they generate some consideration and perhaps some enrichment of life, of Scripture, and of love.

FOREWORD

In the old movie *Grand Canyon*, Danny Glover tells his friend about his trips to the Grand Canyon. Danny plays the part of a character who lives in the ghetto somewhere on the East Coast. He lives surrounded by dirt, drugs, poverty, and hopelessness. He works hard just to keep himself afloat. About once a year, he confides in his friend, he makes a trip to the Grand Canyon. The man asks why. "I leave here and go out there and sit on the edge of that huge chasm and just look. Just look as far as the eye can see. And it takes my breath away. I see something bigger than I am. And I go back home and it helps me make it."

A long time ago, Kris Kristofferson sang plaintively, "Help us make it through the night." We are all in need of some words to help us through the days as well. It's tough out there in this crazy, mixed-up time. We need some reminders to keep us healthy and hopeful.

I've been reading Andrew Smith's stuff for years. Many times I have encouraged him to put the best of his words into a book. Well, here they are. I don't rightly know what to call these pages. They are prayers and meditations and questions and words that come straight from the heart. They are reminders of grace, love, faith, and even hope.

We all need some rememberings to keep us going. I recommend these words to everyone. Don't read them straight through. They should be read slowly and carefully—maybe one each day. They are much like a throat lozenge. You don't gulp these tiny nuggets down—you savor them slowly. These words may make you smile. They may make you cry. But most of all, they will make you think.

Andrew, fine architect, thinking Christian, churchman, good writer, husband, father, and friend—thanks for this graceful gift that you have given us.

Roger Lovette,
Ash Wednesday 2012

REFLECTIONS ON LIFE

AWARENESS

When you feel that God is distant
And not involved in your life—
Rejoice!
Comfort is on its way.

The awareness of need
Is the first step to reconciliation.

God,
The hound of heaven,
Is constantly
Pursuing you,
Wooing you,
Calling you
Into fellowship
And joy.

Praise the Lord!

THEN

Hugh Prather said in, "Notes on love and courage"

"The ponderous broom of history
Sweeping away all traces of
Individual lives motivates you
More than the hope
Of ten thousand golden statues
Or trumpets
Or coins."

When the overwhelming problems
Looming out there in the future
Render the history of individual lives
Into meaningless data

Who is going to care
Whether I loved or not?
Whether I was loved or not?
Who will know about the
        Sacrifice
        Discipline
        Commitment
        Loyalty
        Devotion
        Tenderness
        Joy
        Disappointment
        Happiness
        Grief?

Who is going to care
When it is over,
When I, too, have become
Nameless and forgotten?

I don't know about then,
But I do know about now!

I care!

PUFF

Puff the magic dragon
Sailing with Jackie Paper
Across the starless sea.

Sometimes I think that I am like Jackie—
Sure that there are no stars
Simply because there are a few clouds in my sky.

There is a time to be afraid—
The person who is never afraid is a fool.

The question is always when?
When should I be afraid and
When should I be brave?

Regardless of what anybody says,
That is never an easy question.

So when the storms of life make me go rigid with fear,
I try to remember that Jackie and Puff conquered their fear,
And then Jackie only needed Puff on special occasions.

There are times when I need Puff even now,
Because the storms of life still crash upon me
And for a few moments I think that there are no stars.

But then the clouds move on
And the stars are still there.
Exactly where they have been all along.

THE STRUGGLE

Is it true that the struggle is paramount?
Is the thrill of victory really an illusion?
Is the rightness of purpose the sum of success?
Does it matter whether goals are reached or not?

Yes, it matters!

But falling short of a challenging goal
Is not the same as failing
Because there is honor in the struggle.

In fact, the struggle may be more important than success,
For it is struggle
That ennobles the life of mankind.

TO DWELL IN THE MYSTERY

"To dwell in the mystery."
I used that phrase a long time ago in something I wrote.
To dwell in the mystery long enough to let the Holy Spirit do
his work.

Dwell is almost as important a word as *mystery*.
Dwell implies patience.
You cannot dwell in a hurry.

Unhurried time,
Immersed in mystery,
Grounds you to the eternal.

Wait!
Who wants to wait?
Why not act?

Make a decision!
It is not as easy as it seems.
Waiting sometimes takes more strength than action.

Lord, give me patience.
Lord, give me wisdom.
Lord, let me dwell in your mystery.

JOY THAT OVERTAKES SORROW

Karl Barth, in his marvelous little book on Wolfgang Amadeus Mozart, said that Mozart's music had a way "in which joy overtakes sorrow without extinguishing it."

Life must go on, and we must let joy subdue the sorrows that are a natural part of life.

If there was no striving for a higher level of joy, there would be no sorrow; or in reverse, if there was no sorrow, there would be no reason to strive for joy.

Disappointment and sorrow are a natural and appropriate part of life, but joy must prevail.

SMALL GIFTS

Thank you, Lord,
For friends
Who honor us
With small gifts
Of tenderness.

Gifts so freely given
That they cost the giver
Almost nothing
But are of infinite value
To those who receive them.

THE TRANSLATOR

The understanding of all that is "Other"
    is totally dependent
    on the translator!

Cosmic Power,
Divine Initiative,
Primeval Existence,
Essential Being,
Holy God,
    and all such concepts
    are
    —and should be—
    beyond understanding.

Except
    that in Jesus Christ
    we have been given a translator.

It must be significant then
    that the vehicle of that translation
    was human.

He was born of woman.
He was taught as a child.
He was trained as a young man.

He was hungry.
He was tired.
He was afraid.

He was angry.
He was happy.
He was sad.

He was compassionate.
He was loved
And He loved.

Little children,
Young rulers,
Fishermen,

Mary,
Lazarus,
John,

The ten lepers,
The woman at the well,
The woman taken in adultery.

He loved his mother,
        even though He was upset with her
        when she tried to interfere with his life.

He was driven by his sense of mission,
He was misunderstood,
He was abused,

He was ridiculed,
He was mistreated
And finally He was crucified.

We must not forget
        that He was just as much human
        as He was divine.

And because He was translator,
        His relationship to humanity was just as important
        as His relationship to God.

In His humanity He expressed the divine,
and in His divinity He expressed humanity
in its highest form.

Could it be
that in this process of translation,
humanity and divinity became one and the same?

And could it be
that we are just as responsible
to serve as translators of God's love
to those who touch our lives
as He was responsible
for translating God's love
to first-century Judea?

And could it be
that a similar mixture
of humanity and divinity
is just as operative
in our lives as it was in His?

God help us!

ERASURES

The erasures—
The crossed-out words—
The X'd-out paragraphs.

They are so important,
They are the record of change,
They are the beginning of improvement.

If there are no erasures,
there is no improvement.

The manuscript tells so much more than the finished page. The starts—the stops—the blind alleys—the deletions—the wrong turns—the turn-arounds—the deliberate reversals of direction.

It is like the word picture from the Yoruba language that Dr. Scott Patterson used to explain the concept of repentance:

"A man who meets himself coming down the road."

Why do we hide the erasures?
Why do we leave out the blanked-out words?
Why do we ignore the X'd-out paragraphs?

They tell us so much.
They remind us that we have changed.
They encourage us to continue to make changes.

Erasures prepare us to grow in the Kingdom of God.

MUSIC IN THE SUFFERING

None of us are immune to suffering and grief.

The question is, "How well do we live our lives in times of trouble?"

Paul in the book of Corinthians tells us about the suffering he experienced. He was jailed, beaten, stoned, whipped, ship wrecked and abused in many ways. Paul knew what it is was to suffer but later, in the book of Romans, he talked about hope and suffering.

How can he mix those two words?

How can he link them together?

Paul knew that there was no promise of relief from suffering simply because he was a Christian. He knew that the will of God would not erase the dark times.

It is during the difficult times that God fills us with hope.

Hope is what fills the vacuum left by disappointment and loss.

Hope does not disappoint us.

Hope brings assurance.

Hope develops perseverance.

Hope evolves into patience.

Hope that is seen and understood is not hope.

Marten Luther King said, "We must accept finite disappointment but we must believe in infinite hope".

Havel said, "Hope is not the conviction that something will turn out well but that there will be meaning in whatever happens."

A person of hope can hear music in the suffering.

THE WALL

There are times when we run smack into the wall of reality.
Times, when we realize that there will not be enough time.
That we will not be able to do everything we planned to do.

The fact is that there is never enough time.
Adequate time is a luxury; an illusion of youth.
There are always more dreams and hopes than there is time.

Time is the common currency of all people.
All we can do is to use the time we have wisely.
Neither allegiance to false hope or flight from reality will add
time to our lives.

The only option we have is quality.
We can change the quality of our lives.
We can use it to celebrate the love of God and share that love
with others.

TIME

In this age of scientific precision—
When the movements of the far reaches
Of the universe are charted
To mere fractions of a second,

It is significant that time
That is truly important
Is never measured by the chronograph
Or disciplined by the metronome.

When time has been tempered by the reality of life
And steeped with the emotions of the human heart,
Normal rhythms and pace get out of synch—
And some seconds last longer than others.

There is no rationale for the compression of time
That can make our earliest memories as fresh as yesterday
Or for the elongation of time
That can make one tender moment last a lifetime.

    Like the three second kiss
    That is tasted for fifty years
    Or the single smile of acceptance
    That beams forever like the light of an eternal flame.

    Like the month long days
    That seem to never end
    The week before the wedding vows
    Are actually spoken.

    Like the decade spent in the little room
    At the front of the church

Waiting for the musical cue that will beckon you
To come out and see your bride walk down the aisle.

Like the minute it take for a babe in arms
To grow into a teenager
Flushed with the joy
Of being in love for the first time.

Like the day that passes so quickly
In which your parents change
From vigorous providers and protectors
To sage but enfeebled elders of the tribe.

Like the year that flies by so swiftly
Between the wedding and the silver anniversary
And the year or two more
Until the silver turns to gold.

Thank you God for giving us hearts
That sustain us when time stands still
And enshrines forever,
Time that sanctifies our very existence.

REFLECTIONS ON CHRISTMAS

IMMANUEL

There are a few times
When we are honest enough to admit
That we do not understand
Why you came as a baby
Cradled in a manger.

Why couldn't you have continued to be
A God of anger
Like you were
When the children of Israel
Built the golden calf?

Why couldn't you have remained
A God of power
Like you were
When you zapped
The altar for Elijah?

Why couldn't you have stayed
A God of mystery
Like you were
When you sent the plague
On Sennacherib's army?

We could understand you
When you revealed yourself as
      A God of anger,
      A God of power,
      A God of mystery.
But how do we cope with a God
Who comes with the humility
Of a new born babe?

It was
>So undignified,
>So unspectacular,
>So common,
To be born
Like all other human beings!

Does the commonness of your coming
Mean that the love of God
Can flow through common people like us
Just like it flowed through you?

Is it true
That we too
Must be,
"Immanuel"
"God with us"
To a lost and dying world?

Grant that this celebration of your birth
Might humble us
Like you were humbled in Bethlehem
And that through that humbleness
Your kingdom might prosper on this earth.

HELPLESSNESS

The helplessness of the infant
implies that God has not
given up on this world.

It is the human process;
>   birth
>   growth
>   learning
>   living
>   sharing
>   ministering
>   dying
that the WORD of God was operative—then—
in the person of Jesus Christ.

That the WORD of God is operative—now—
in your life and mine.

Immanuel—God with us—
is still the "Good News"
for all mankind!

A SLOW CHRISTMAS

Sometimes it seems
That we should slow down
The celebration
Of Christmas.

It seems that
Every year
The pace gets faster
And faster.

Parties,
Ballgames,
Dinners,
Shopping,
Concerts,
Trees,
Gifts.

Our total existence
Seems to be
A series
Of special events.

But

In the midst
Of all the
Festivity
And frivolity

And froth
We are painfully aware
That life goes on.

Surgery is still scheduled,
Children are still hungry,
Lovers are still estranged,
The elderly are still lonely,
The homeless are still cold,
People are still unemployed,
Tragedy still strikes
And war rumbles
In many places on this earth.

Slow us down—
Slow us down enough to remember
That the significance
Of the first Christmas
Was the simple birth of a child.

Slow us down—
Slow us down until we realize
That the first Christmas
Has no meaning
Unless we too experience Emmanuel.

And when we are finally quite
Remind us that the Emmanuel
That counts
Is the Emmanuel
The world sees in us.

Grant that the peace
That only you can bring
Will be infused into our lives

And that Christmas
Will be more than
Festivity
And frivolity
And froth.

Perhaps we should
Pray for a
Slow Christmas.

CHRISTMAS GLASSES

Jesus,
Do you understand
Why we have changed
The celebration
Of your birth
Into a pantheon
Of pagan symbols
And practices?

What does Santa Claus
Have to do with Bethlehem?
Wasn't the story
Of the three wise men
Enough to establish
A tradition
Of giving gifts?

And where did we
Get the idea
Of giving gifts
To each other?
I thought
The wise men
Brought their
Gifts to you.

And the Christmas tree—
Where is the verse
In Luke that tells
About the shepherds
Bringing a fir tree
Into the stable?

Was the Bethlehem star
So insignificant
That we had to invent
A tree for it
To sit on?

A tree
With tinsel
And baubles
And trinkets
And fake icicles
That probably looks
More like something
Out of a Persian market
Than a part
Of the stables of Bethlehem.

And all those
Other ridiculous symbols
That dilute
The holiness
Of the Christmas event.

A reindeer with a red nose,
Elves that work at the north pole,
Gingerbread men
And toy soldiers.
Parades
And ballgames
And cocktail parties
And open houses
And all kinds
Of holiday festivities.

Or the endless string
Of silly sentimental songs—
White Christmas,
Blue Christmas,
Jingle Bells,
Sleigh Bells,
Christmas Bells,
Chestnuts on the Fire,
And days of French hens
And partridges in pear trees
And winter wonderlands
And drummer boys
And talking toys.
Being home for Christmas
With mamma kissing Santa Claus
And the whole gang
Rocking around the Christmas Tree.

Where is
The awe
The wonder
The magnificence
The holiness
The joy
Of Emmanuel?

Are we
So blind
So stupid
So careless
So pagan
That we do not know
What Emmanuel means?

God with us!
God is with us!

Jesus
You probably
Do understand
The weakness
Of our humanity—
You know
That we are afraid
Of the sublime
Of the holy
Of the mystery.

We do not
Want to
Get too close!

We must
Have some
Distance!

We must have
Our pagan symbols
And practices.

We must have
A shield
From the awesome truth
Revealed in your coming.

We are not ready
For you to be
"With us!"

Jesus
Would you happen
To have
Some of those
Special eye glasses?
The kind with
Filter lenses?

Lenses that
Filter out
The pagan symbols
That have corrupted
The celebration
Of your birth.

Jesus
We do not want
You to take away
Our pagan symbols.

We need
Our illusions
And our myths.

We cannot give up
The dancing eyes
And racing hearts
Of our little ones
Waiting for the sound
Of reindeer hooves
As they go to sleep
On Christmas eve.

And we have established
Warm and meaningful
Traditions around

The Christmas tree—
The tree topped
With a star
Or by an angel—
With lights
And trinkets
And ornaments
And a pile
Of presents.

Some of us have
Giving spirits
At Christmas
Even though the
Rest of the year
Is dominated
By cold hearts
And miserly spirits.

We have learned
To love the carols—
And we even like
The silly sentimental songs!

Christmas is the
Most musical time
Of our year.
Music is everywhere!

Symphony orchestras,
High school bands
And even rock and roll bands
All have their versions
of Christmas songs.
Church choirs,
Youth choirs

And groups
Of little children
Present plays
And pageants
And musical programs
Of every kind.

Opera singers
Who sing loud and verbose,
Blues singers
Who sing mournful and slow,
Country singers
Who sing with nasal tones and broken hearts
And even those of us
Who cannot sing at all
Sing the songs
Of Christmas
And make off key
Humming noises
While we work.

We find ourselves
Listening to Christmas music
All day long
Even if it is
Silly
And sentimental
Or even pagan.

Jesus
Let us keep
Our pagan ways
Of celebrating
Your birth
But let us
Also keep

Those special glasses
With the filter lenses
So we can
See for just
A little while

The awe,
The wonder,
The magnificence,
The holiness
And the joy
Of Emmanuel!

US!

For unto us a child is given—
Unto us!
Us!

Us—
Who are not worthy,
Who are not grateful,
Who are not responsive.

But a child is given—
Given anyway—
Regardless.

The universal symbol of hope—
New life,
New opportunity,
New relationship.

The universal object of love—
As soft as a new mother's coos.
As natural as a baby finding his mother's breast.

How else could a God of love identify with mankind?
How else could it be, "God is with us?"

THE BABY

"And all who heard it were amazed . . ."

Luke 2:18

What am I going to do
with this baby?

I didn't expect this much responsibility;
these demands; this anxiety.

Those shepherds said that they were amazed.
They don't know anything!

Somehow I am going to do it.
I didn't ask for this baby
but God has chosen me to be His mother
and I am going to do the very best I can.

The question is what are we twentieth century Christians
going to do with this baby!

Whatever we do, we are going to do it here; now.
Here and now where choice or destiny has placed us.

The salvation of the world is in our hands.
What are we going to do with it?

Will we, like Mary,
be able to treasure in our hearts
the events of our encounter
with the God of Bethlehem?

MARY'S REFLECTIONS

"O, little town of Bethlehem,
How still we see thee lie!"

Bethlehem, place of anticipation;

> "I thought we would never get here. I would have stayed home if I had known how difficult the journey would be. It wasn't easy to ride a donkey in my condition."

Bethlehem, place of anxiety;

> "I didn't know what to expect. My mother didn't tell me very much. Of course she and the village midwife expected to be with me when the baby came."

Bethlehem, place of rejection;

> "I couldn't believe they had no room at the inn! At least the stable was private. He didn't have to be born in a room with a lot of strangers."

Bethlehem, place of pain;

> "I wasn't ready for the pain. When the pains started I thought, 'This is not so bad,' but I sure was wrong about that. I sure am glad it is over."

Bethlehem, place of fear;

> "Those crusty old shepherds must have nearly died of fright when the Angel appeared to them! I still don't understand everything that happened."

Bethlehem, place of wonder;

> "A heavenly chorus? Glory to God in the highest and on earth peace, good will toward men? My baby? It is still too wonderful to comprehend!"

Bethlehem, place of joy;

> "Tidings of great joy. That is what the shepherds said the angel said. I knew that the baby would be special but I certainly did not expect all this attention."

Bethlehem, place of amazement;

> "He sure is a pretty baby. Look how eager he is for my milk. My life sure has changed; a year ago I was a carefree girl and now look at me!"

Bethlehem, place of responsibility;

> "Joseph and I are going to have to take care of this baby. We will have to raise him in the will of God so he can do what he was sent to do."

Bethlehem, place of hope;

> "I must remember these feelings of great expectation. Surely God will show me why all these wonderful things have happened to me. I am so full of hope."

> *"The hopes and fears of all the years,*
> *Are met in thee tonight."*

Reflections by Andrew
"O little town of Bethlehem" by Philip Brooks

JOSEPH'S REFLECTIONS

*"When they finished everything . . . .
they returned to Galilee to . . . ."*

Luke 2:39

Gone,
All those special events,
Finished,
Over,
Gone!

The star,
The angels,
The shepherds,
The wise men,
Faded away,
Vanished into the heavens.

No more heavenly host,
No more midnight messengers,
No more prophetic utterances.
Even the gifts had to be spent
to finance the trip to Egypt.

Gone,
All those special events
Are gone.
It's back to normal now,
Back to the reality of living.

Well, not quite normal,
At least not like it was when we left Nazareth.

Now I've got a wife and a baby to take care of.
Now it is up to me.
I can't expect help from angels, wise men and shepherds anymore.

I hope my old friends remember me.
Surely there is still a need for a good carpenter.
I wonder where I left my hammer and saw?

Surely God will not desert us now.
Surely he will watch over us.
Surely goodness and mercy will follow us.

I will have to remember the prophet Isaiah said:

> *"I will trust and not be afraid,*
> *for the Lord God is my strength*
> *and my might . . . ."*

Isaiah 12:2

It's going to take a lot of hard work to feed and clothe this little family but I'm not afraid of hard work.

I wonder if this little fellow will have a carpenter's skills in his hands? He is such a special child. I wonder if God has something else planned for him.

A rabbi?
A priest?
A prophet?

I can't worry about that now.
I've got to get some new contracts.
I've got to get this carpentry shop back in order.

Those days Bethlehem,
They sure were special,
God certainly was with us,
I wonder what it all means.

But life can't be special events all the time.
I'd better stop this day dreaming and get to work.
God we are depending on you.

"And the child grew and became strong . . . ."

Luke 2:39

LET'S GO . . . .

"And suddenly there was with the angel a multitude of the heavenly hosts praising god, and saying, glory to God in the highest, and on earth peace, good will toward men."

Luke 2:13 & 14

Peace on earth?
Goodwill to men?
What do they mean?
Do they really expect us to believe that?

There never has been peace on earth—
not since Cain killed Abel!

Every story we have heard
has been about conflict
and war
and pain
and death.

The patriarchs of old
clawed and fought
every day for a place to live—
and then came
the Egyptians
the Canaanites
the Philistines

the Ammonites
the Moabites
the Babylonians
the Chaldeans
the Greeks
and now the terrible Romans.

They all extracted
the sweat of our brows
the blood of our bodies
and the essence of our souls.

How can we believe
that there is going to be
Peace on Earth?

How do we know
we are not suffering
from a skin of bad wine?

Peace on Earth?
Goodwill to men?

How wonderful it sounds!
How wonderful it would be!

Can it be?
Can we trust?
Can we hope?
Can we even dream?

Are we going to let ourselves
be trapped into another futile round of hope?

Haven't we seen hope
and dreams

and expectations
dashed into the ground
over and over again?

But how can we ignore a message from Angles?
How can we forget the Heavenly Hosts?

How can we give up hope?
How can we not believe?

Let's go,
Let's go into Bethlehem
and see what the Lord God hath wrought!

So they went—
not knowing—
full of questions—
scared to hope—
scared to not hope—
overcome by the awesome events—
expecting who knows what?

And what did they find?
A baby!
A newborn child.
Wrapped in swaddling clothes!

God's ultimate expression of love!
God's statement that he has not given up!
God's assurance that he is with us!

Emanuel!
God with us then.
God with us now.

Thank god!

REJOICE—THERE IS HOPE!

"Fear not: for behold, I bring you good tidings of great joy . . ."

Luke 2:10

Rejoice!
    No more war.
    Peace on earth.
No—Not yet.
But there is hope.

Rejoice!
    Poverty is gone.
    The good life for everyone.
No—Not yet.
But there is hope.

Rejoice!
    A long and healthy life for all.
    Sickness and pain are no more.
No—Not yet.
But there is hope.

Rejoice!
    Anxiety and fear have vanished.
    Depression does not lurk in the darkness.
No—Not yet.
But there is hope.

Rejoice!
    The fountain of youth is flowing.
    The debilitating ravages of old age are no more.

No—Not yet.
But there is hope.

Rejoice!
> Racism is a thing of the past.
> The color of a person's skin in of no concern

No—Not yet.
But there is hope.

Rejoice!
> Ethic hatred is history.
> Brother does not hate brother.

No—Not Yet.
But there is hope.

Rejoice!
> Generosity rules the day.
> Greed has given way to benevolence.

No—Not yet.
But there is hope.

Rejoice!
> The wolf also shall dwell with the lamb
> And the leopard shall lie down with the kid.

No—Not yet.
But there is hope.

Yes—There is hope!
> God has sent his son.
> Emmanuel—God is with us.

Rejoice!

REFLECTIONS ON EASTER

WHY?

"He set his face to go to Jerusalem . . ."

Luke 9:51

Jesus . . . .
Why were you so determined to go to Jerusalem?
You could have spent at least one more year teaching and healing the sick!

Why force confrontation?
Why invite certain trouble?
Why make a dramatic entry?
Why call attention to conflict?
Why attack the bear in his den?
Why was it so important to do it then?
Why wave a red flag in the face of the bull?

Why not heal more people?
Why not win more tax collectors?
Why not multiply more loves and fishes?
Why not teach more about the Kingdom?
Why not retreat one more time to the mountain?
Why not spend more time with the twelve disciples?
Why not preach to thousands and thousands more Galileans?

Why does the story say nothing about the happy times?
There must have been some good times mixed in with the bad.

What about the meals?
What about the sunrises?
What about the Sunsets?

What about the flowers?
What about the campfires?
What about the quite talks?
What about the little children?

Why pain?
Why betrayal?
Why the cross?
Why the disappointment?
Why do we hear about your grief?
Why do we hear about your anguish?
Why does it have to end in your death?

Why did you set your face to go to Jerusalem?
Why did you go with such determination and drive?

Was it because you knew that total love gives everything?
Was it because you knew that life without sacrifice is meaningless?
Was it because of the divine imperative that, "All things must be fulfilled?"
Was it because, "If I be lifted up from the earth I will draw all men unto me?"
Was it because you knew that ultimate obedience does not shrink from danger?
Was it because, "For the joy that was set before you, you would endure the cross?"

Why did you love us enough to die on the cross?

We do not understand why.
We only know that you did.

HE WEPT

"As he came near and saw the city, he wept . . . ."

Luke 19:41

A God who weeps!

It's incredulous!
It's illogical!
It's unbelievable!
But there he is,
Weeping over Jerusalem.

Why?
Why should he weep?
They were not going to change.
They were simply doing what they had always done.
They had been killing their prophets for a thousand years.
Even those who repented and were baptized by John
were nowhere to be found as the specter of the cross came into
focus.

A God who cares!
He knew what kind of people they were.
Arrogant,
Proud,
Stubborn,
They did not want to hear anything new.
They did not want change.

The signs,
The miracles,
The parables,

They were wonderful.
They were amazing.
They were the fulfillment of prophecy,
But the Jews were not about to change!

A God who is touched by the pain of man!
What tragedy they heap upon their heads.
What disasters their rebellion will bring.
What conflict lies in store for them,

So unnecessary,
So inevitable,
So tragic.

Only a weeping God could go into that city,
        into the jaws of death.
Only after he had exhausted his weeping
        could he be resolute in his time of trial.
Only after his emotions had been used up
        could he be, "As a sheep before his shearers is dumb."
Only a weeping God could deliberately sacrifice himself for
        people who were ungrateful,
        who were unrepentant,
        who were unworthy.

Some people like to think of God sitting on a golden throne,
judging the nations of the world,

But for me it is
The caring God,
The touched God,
The emotional God,
The weeping God,
That demands my loyalty,
My all.

A God who weeps!

It's incredulous!
It's illogical!
It's unbelievable!

But there he is
Weeping over me!

For here I am,
Arrogant,
Proud,
Stubborn,
Ungrateful,
Unrepentant,
Unworthy,

But still he cares for me.
But still he is touched by my pain.
And still he weeps over my sin.

"As he came near and saw the city, he wept . . . ."

> "Oh, how I love Jesus,
> Oh, how I love Jesus,
> Oh, how I love Jesus,
> Because he 'wept' for me"

PANIC!

"And he sent Peter and John saying, 'Go and prepare us the Passover that we may eat' ".

Luke 22:8

So Peter looked around the room to be sure that everything was ready—
And whispered to John with a little panic in his voice,

"Where is that foot washing servant?"

The lamb is ready.
The wine is ready.
The bread is ready.
Everything is ready.

"Where is that foot washing servant?"

The Master is here.
The guests are here.
The towels are here.
The basin of water is here.

"Where is that foot washing servant?"

Somebody has got to wash our feet.
I'm not going to do it!
It's not dignified.
It's not my job!

"Where is that foot washing servant?"

"He took off his robe and tied the towel around himself."

Not my feet!
What is he doing?
He's not going to wash our feet!
He's not going to do the job of the foot washing servant.

"Where is that foot washing servant?"

"If I don't wash you, you have no part of me?"

The foot washing servant.
Peter found the foot washing servant.
The Lord was the foot washing servant!

"Lord, not only my feet but also my hands and my head."

What a surprise!
What an example!
What a challenge!

Can we become servants?
Can we be humble?
Can we be like Jesus?

Shock us Lord.
Shock us like you shocked Peter.
Teach us to be humble.

EVERY ONE?

" . . . He said, verily I say unto you, that one of you shall betray me. And they . . . began every one of them to say unto him, is it I"?

Matthew 26:21 and 22

Every one of them?
Surely not Andrew and Phillip!
Surely not Peter, James and John!
Surely not every one of them!

Judas was the obvious one—wasn't he?
The zealot was the one with the twisted mind—wasn't he?
The brooding, contrary, recalcitrant one—wasn't he?
Why did every one of them say, "Is it I?"

John the beloved?
Did John have within his heart the potential to betray his master?
Were there circumstances that could change the beloved into the betrayer?
Was it fear and doubt that compelled John to say, "Is it I?"

Impetuous Peter!
We know that later Peter's brashness would get him into trouble.
We know that later Peter would be guilty of denial.
Was that the character trait that made Peter say, "Is it I?"

Judas must have been ugly and sinister—wasn't he?
He must have been freighting like Vincent Price or Boris Karloff.

Or he might have been sinister like Peter Lorie or James Cagney.

It was natural for him to be evil but why did the others say, "Is it I?"

What was it in the hearts of the other eleven that made them say, "Is it I?"

Did they all know that they had within them the potential for betrayal?

Did they all know that fear and uncertainty can result in strange behavior?

Did they all realize that sin and guilt is never far away?

Could it be that they all knew that they were sinful men?

Could it be that they all knew that failure is one temptation away?

Could it be that Judas was not ugly, sinister and freighting?

Could it be that they were sincere when they asked, "Is it I?"

Perhaps there is more than enough sin in all of us.

Perhaps there is the possibility of failure in all of us.

Perhaps betrayal is not restricted to the ugly, sinister and freighting.

Perhaps we should all say with the twelve, "Is it I?"

YOU SOUND LIKE HIM!

"And Peter . . . . warmed himself by the fire . . . . and a maid said, Surely thou are one of them: for thou art a Galilean, and thy speech agreeth thereto."

Mark 14:54, 69 and 70

You are a Galilean.
You are one of them.
You sound like him!

He was warming by the wrong fire.
His motives were a little twisted.
He was in trouble before he knew it.

But;

He couldn't disguise who he was.
He couldn't deny where he had been.
He couldn't hide what he had been doing.

You sound like him!

He had seen too many miracles.
He had heard too many parables.
He had been close to Jesus too long.

When the pressure overcame him,
He swore that he had never known him,
But he was unconvincing;
He had been too close, too long.

Jesus knew;

He knew the intimacy of the past,
He knew the failure of the present,
He knew the glory of the future.

Later; after the resurrection,
Jesus said, "Go tell the disciples
And also tell Peter".

Tell Peter that the tomb is open.
Tell Peter that I am alive.
Tell Peter that I love him.

But what about us?

We too have our moments of failure.
We too have our time of denial.
We too have our nights warming by the wrong fire.

But;

Does our speech betray us?
Does our action tell on us?
Does the world know that we have been close to Jesus?

We are like Peter;

The question is not where we have been.
The question is where we are.
The question is where are we going?

What are we going to do after we have warmed by the wrong fire?
What are we going to do after we have denied him?
What are we going to do after the cock has crowed?

That is the question!

FORCED LABOR!

"And as they came out, they found a man of Cyrene, Simon by name: him they compelled to bear his cross."

Matthew 27:32

He made his way to the edge of the street.
He looked to see this so called prophet from Galilee.
He wanted to know why everybody was so excited.

And then it happened!

"You, you there! Pick up that cross and follow him!"

Forced labor!

He didn't volunteer.
He didn't intend to get involved.
He didn't want to be anything but a spectator.

But there he was dragging a heavy cross up a mountain,
following a beaten, disheveled, bloody man,
listening to the ridicule, the taunts, the abuse.

Forced Labor!

Forced to do the dirty work.
Forced to carry the cross for a condemned man.
Forced to be a participant instead of a spectator.

Sometimes the course of our lives
is determined by reason, by planning, by logic.
We analyze the data, we look at the facts, we consider the
options
and move forward with confidence and assurance

We do it! We do it because it is right.

Sometimes the course of our lives is determined by a call,
by an overwhelming sense of need, by a challenge.
It is not something we have planned.
It is not even logical.

But we do it! We do it because we can not ignore the call!

Sometimes the course of our lives is determined by what is
forced upon us!
We simply happen to be in a particular place at a point in time
and there is a demand beyond our control.
Circumstances or fate puts a task into our hands that is totally
unexpected.

But we do it. We do it because we have no choice but to do it!

Forced labor!

Sometimes the course of our lives is shaped by reason and
logic.
Sometimes the course of our lives is shaped by a call.
Sometimes the course of our lives is shaped by what is forced
upon us.

Simon of Cyrene carried the cross for our Savior.
He may or may not have known that he was part
of the most significant event in history, but he did what he was
forced to do.

May we be diligent in our planning for service.
May we listen prayerfully for God's call.
May we rejoice in the tasks that are forced upon us.

How we respond to the opportunity to serve,
regardless the way it is revealed to us
is what makes us what we are.

CRUCIFY HIM!

Jesus, it is every difficult
To pray a public prayer on Easter Sunday morning
Because the very sinus of my soul
Are racked with the guilt of your cross.

It was my greed and selfishness
That cried, "CRUCIFY HIM, CRUCIFY HIM!"

It was my anger and frustration
That drove the nails into your hands

And it was my fear and insecurity
That left you to die—alone!

Though the public part of this prayer is difficult,
The corporate part is easy,
Because Mary, Stephen, Beverly, Jim, Dorothy, Bob;
All my friends were there,
They all helped me.

All we can do is cry,
Forgive us for we did not know what we were doing.
Forgive us for what we did then;
Forgive us for what we are doing now.

We are sill greedy;
We want more than our fair share of this world's goods.

We are still selfish;
We care only for our own happiness.

We are still frustrated;
We cannot accept our own limitations;

We are still afraid;
We do not want to suffer and we do not want to die.

Help us, Oh Jesus, to remember
That you did not stay on the cross;
That you did not remain in the grave;

That all the evil of this world did not defeat you
And that the empty tomb is our symbol of hope.

Take away the guilt that fills our souls
And saturate us with the spirit of your resurrection.

THE JOY OF RESURRECTION

"He is not here; he has risen."

Matthew 28:6

Jesus, every time we think we have it all figured out,
  A tornado sweeps down from the sky,
  Chemotherapy continues its steady drip,
  The surgeon's knife begins to cut on flesh,
  Or fate in some other way strikes without mercy.

Jesus, help us to remember that on the first Easter.
  You came out of the grave.
  You left the shroud in the tomb.
  You conquered the pain and sting of death.
  You descended into hell and returned victorious.

May the joy of your resurrection
Infuse our celebration of Easter.
And may the power of your victory over evil
Enable us to face the uncertainties this life
With both confidence and humility.

CRASHING THE PARTY

"when the doors were shut where the disciples were assembled for fear of the Jews, Jesus came and stood in the midst . . ."

John 20:19

Ten disciples were gathered in an upper room.

"Do you really believe that he is alive?"
  "Mary saw him!"
    "Mary is so emotional."
      "She is so sensitive."
        "She is so impressionable."
          "We can't believe her, can we?

"Lock those doors."
  "You never know who might be a traitor!"
    "We never suspected Judas, did we?
      "What are we going to do?"
        "We can't do anything without him."
          "We might as well go fishing."

Then he came through the door and changed everything.
They were not looking for him.
He was unexpected, uninvited.

He crashed the party!
He crashed the party!

The grace of God is not a matter of what we want.
It is not what we expect.
It is the gift of God.

It is God with us—Emmanuel—not only in Bethlehem but also in a locked room full of frightened and confused men.

It is God with us—Emmanuel—In the locked hearts of twenty-first century men and women who are frightened and confused.

He crashed the party!
He crashed it then and he wants to crash it now.

Open the door and let him in!

REFLECTIONS ON LOVE

BLOODY FEET

When I was young
I knew exactly where I was going—
I was sure I was going to win the race!

But I got lost along the way—
The path was full of briars and stones—
I walk slowly now and my feet are bloody.

But I have discovered that he miracle of life
is that even with bloody feet
I can still love!

The direction is not what I dreamed,
It is not what I thought reasonable,
but I can still love.

It is not the love that lives in my reverie—
the pure, free, joyous love of youth,
but I can still love.

The love that goes with bloody feet
Is more akin to struggle,
to task,
to commitment,
but it is still love.

And I have learned that bloody feet
        Do not destroy the déjà vu of love,
        They do not deter the dream of love.
        They do not deny the opportunity to love,

In fact bloody feet do not hurt now
nearly as much as they used to.

THE NEED

What is the common need
of all mankind?

"To give and receive
a little tenderness."

TOUGH LOVE

It is interesting to contemplate the mental aspect of our relationship to God. Christianity is traditionally thought of as a condition of the heart and the heart is thought of as the seat of the emotions. However; in many ways Christianity is a condition of the mind that allows our lives to be open to the power of God. The mind is the instrument that allows for the open life.

It takes an incredible amount of self-discipline to accept the risks involved in openness. It is true that the Holy Spirit, working through the heart, the seat of the emotions, enhances such things as compassion and love and joy and caring and consideration and tenderness, but it is the mind that generates the mental toughness that can produce deliberate love. It is mental love, agape love that enables us to love the unlovely. The love described in the 13th Chapter of I Corinthians has nothing to do with passion—it has everything to do with mental love—tough love.

The love of God is deliberate; is given without consideration of merit; is given without expectation of reciprocity. Love for others must also be given without consideration of merit—otherwise it would be impossible for us to love our enemies. We love God with all our hearts (emotionally) because we know of his love as expressed in His Word and we have experienced his love through His salvation and we have felt His love in the fellowship of His Church. We love the unlovely because we have been taught by the example of Jesus on the cross sacrificing himself for all mankind. "God so loved the world that He gave His only begotten Son . . . ."—deliberately; Gave because He wanted to; Gave because He willed Himself to give; Gave because of a mental action not because of an emotional reaction.

We too must give deliberately—thoughtfully—willfully without regard for success—not for reciprocity or reward. Mental love—risky love—tough love!

COMMITMENT

Something strange and wonderful happens
When you stop and contemplate the difference
Between love and commitment.

When we were young it was so easy to say I love you.
It was even easier to say it
When it was a substitute for saying I want you.
In retrospect it is impossible to know whether it was
I love you therefore I want you or
I want you therefore I love you.

Sometimes it seems
That all the significant happenings of our lives
Are directed by our glans!
The desire for sexual fulfillment is so strong
That love and want are seldom separated
When decisions about love are made!

It is only later
When the initial fires of passion have been dampened by
reality-
When disappointment, failure, heartache and grief
Have become just as much a part of life
As love, passion and orgasm—
Only then does time permit—if we are lucky
The surrender of both love
And passion to commitment.

Commitment is different than love or passion.
Commitment—true commitment—
Commitment born in the midst of despair,

Is a function of the head,
It is a product of thought,
It is the result of reason.

Love can be inflamed by the palpitations of the heart
And passion is driven by the flow of juices to the groin,
But commitment can look both love and passion in the eye
And know the difference between reality and fantasy!

I know that my, "I love yous,"
Have been lived out incompletely
And that my, "I want yous,"
Have been expressed awkwardly.
And I know that your love,
Which I expected to be divine,
Is just as imperfect as mine.

In fact it seems at times
That the dominate force
That flows between us
Is imperfection!

I know that there are gaps
Between us that will never be bridged
And that there are issues
Upon which we will never agree.
But I have also lived long enough
To discover that Camelot never did exist!

It always was a fantasy!

Therefore, commitment that is deliberately given—
Given in the light of a lifetime of both joy and despair
Is in its own way
Stronger than love and sweeter than passion.

IMPERFECTION

Imperfection is all around us!
Everywhere!

We must not allow ourselves to be dominated by the
imperfect.
Remember that our hope for the perfect is the very means
by which we recognize the imperfect.

If we did not know what is best,
Or if we did not care what is best,
We would not be in such a desperate struggle.

Faith in,
And hope for improvement
Is the essence of what traditional Christians call salvation.

The Good News is that we do not have to remain as we are!
        Racked by guilt,
        Paralyzed by fear.
We can improve,
And it is love that provides the courage to challenge the
imperfect
And live with it.

The imperfect in many cases can be dealt with,
And in any case it can be lived with,
But we must not fool ourselves,
It will never go away.

To be human means that imperfection is a part of life,
But to be loved means that imperfection can be faced with
courage.

The fact that God loves us and understands our imperfection
is what theologians call Justification!

The goal of love is,
      To redeem,
      To improve,
      To make right,
      To embrace,
      To cherish,
      To celebrate joy
And all of this takes hard work
And massive risks!

This is what we have been taught by scripture.
God in Christ brought love to mankind,
And it took
      Hard work,
      Massive risks,
      And total sacrifice,
And that is what history calls the Cross!

It is not what we have been,
Or what we are,
But what we can be that makes the difference.

What we can be;
Changed by the love of God;
Sanctified by His love flowing through us.

We are becoming,
We will always be becoming,
Which means that we haven't made it yet,

We will never be perfect,
We will always have to deal with the imperfect.
We will never stop loving.

TO GIVE LOVE
TO RECEIVE LOVE
TO BE LOVED
TO FEEL LOVED

How can facets of the same experience—
The same emotion be so distinct?
Can this alloy of loves
Which are so inseparable,
Also be alien to each other?

Is the struggle to find a balance
Within the varied forms of love
The driving force of our lives
And is it true that most of us
Settle for less than complete harmony?

What is the affliction
That makes fulfilling love so hard to find
That some never experience the joy
And so difficult that the rest of us
Know it for only brief periods of time?

Is it the heady wine of idealism?
The illusions of youth?
Or the fantasy of fairy tales
That makes us hold on so tenaciously
To the hope that a consummate love can be found?

Can it be that the heart of the dreamer
Is full of immaturity

And the romantic is simply one who sticks his head in the sand
So that he cannot see
That which is obvious to the more courageous?

Is the love we are searching for
Always present but imprisoned, unreleased and unrealized
Because of a minor short circuit in the giver?
In the receiver?
In both?

Are any of us actually ready
To undergo the ultimate catharsis
Of giving our love away,
Totally and completely?
Don't we all reserve at least a small part for ourselves?

Is it the insensitivity of the receiver
That blocks the flow of love
Or is it the dearth of flow
From the giver
That renders the receiver unreceptive?

Is it the constant probing of the raw place,
That we know so well,
That causes the pain that blocks out expressions,
That under other circumstances,
Would be called love?

Perhaps the numbness that keeps us from feeling loved
Is due to old scars.
Who is the surgeon
Whose scalpel can carve away the dead places
And let love flow again?

Is it you Lord?
I am ready!

I will gladly go under the knife.
It does not matter how radical the surgery may be.
I do not even ask for guaranteed success.

But then surgery is not always the answer
To problems of the heart.
Seldom does the heart respond to the quick cure.
In fact there are many cases where there is no cure—
Except time.

Is the hunger to be loved the illness unto death?
And is the longing for fulfillment
Basic to the fact of our humanity?
Where is the power
That can give us peace to live with reality?

Lord, we know your example of giving love
Because we live with the shame of your cross,
And we know your commandment to love regardless,
But in the weakness of our humanity,
We confess that we need—

TO GIVE LOVE
TO RECEIVE LOVE
TO BE LOVED
TO FEEL LOVED

DEMANDING

One of the
paradoxes of life
is that
while love
is the most demanding
of life's disciplines—
it ceases
to be love
when it becomes
demanding.

THE ENGINE

Sometimes I think that life
Is like the erratic misfiring
Of an engine badly out of tune.

It runs—
It gets you to where you are going—
But it doesn't provide for a lot of ease;
In fact it provides for a lot of anxiety.

But it does get you there,
And if it gets you there
What right do you have to complain?
What promise was there for ease anyway?

We must remember that some engines quit
And all the power in the world
Will not start them again—
And still others misfire forever
And never get to where they are going.

Perhaps the drive of life
Is to get there anyway you can
And the dream of life
Is to have a quite engine!

HAPPINESS

Do not be trapped
Into a futile search for happiness,
For it is both elusive and fleeting.

Rather give yourself, freely,
In unconditional love
To those who need you.

You may find that happiness
Is a by-product of losing yourself
in love for others.

REFLECTIONS AS PRAYER

THE LINE

Lord grant me the ability to see—
Really see—
The opportunities
That life presents to me.

Help me to concentrate
On those opportunities
And respond to them
With eagerness and joy.

Do not destroy
My vision,
My dreams,
My hope.

But do not allow
Me to be so mesmerized
By wishful thinking
That I cannot respond to reality.

Where is the line between
Vision and fantasy,
Dreams and illusion,
Inspiration and madness?

What is this strange excitement
That goes with the risk
Of living on both sides
Of the line?

Give me the courage
To touch both the usual and the unusual,
To look for you in the natural as well as the supernatural,
To hope in spite of the risk of disappointment.

Let me dwell in the mystery long enough
To gather the strength necessary
To minister to the reality
That is all too familiar.

PRAYER

Why is it that when we really need to pray
There are no words?

When life is hanging by a thread,
When death is not a threat but is a reality,
When hope is a word used by visionaries and mystics,
When love's last dying ember has flickered and gone out,
When peace is something left over from a fairy tale,
When a thoughtless, careless act has done irreparable harm,
When adjustments to life that must be made are not made,

Or simply

When a stroke of fate has struck
And we are left with nothing
But tragedy, grief and heartache,

Why is it that at these times, any attempt to pray
Leaves us with words stuck in the base of our throats
And a wave of nausea sweeping across our bodies?

When it really doesn't matter—
When someone picks you out of the crowd
And says,

> "Would you please lead us in a word of prayer?"

We can always stand up and mumble something about—

> "Thank you for this another day,
> Bless us and ours,

Forgive us for our sins.
In Jesus' name. Amen."

And if we have the time
Or the inclination
We can lengthen it,
Polish it,
Embellish it,
Elaborate on it
But when all is said and done we have prayed—

"Thank you for this another day,
Bless us and ours,
Forgive us for our sins.
In Jesus' name. Amen.

But when life
Or hope
Or love is in the balance,
Words of any kind,
No matter how profound,
Seem hollow and cheap
And even gross.

When concern is so deep
That we are sick in the pit of our stomachs,
Elegant words make us want to throw up!

I wonder if that
Is what the Apostle Paul
Was talking about when he said,

"The Spirit itself maketh intercession for us
with groanings which cannot be uttered."

Is it possible
That we do not pray
Until we cannot pray?

Help us our Father
To love with such depth of devotion
That there are no words to convey our feelings,
To hope for the well being of our friends with such fervor
That we are blind to our own needs,
To care with such intensity
That food is unattractive and we fast without realizing it.

Perhaps then we can have the peace of knowing
That we have prayed,
And that you have heard
The unspeakable language of our souls,
And that you have understood our prayer.

SERIOUS

Our Heavenly Father, we come into your presence this morning humbled because we have learned once again how brief life can be.

Sometimes it seems like we stumble through life thinking that we are in control. Wondering from one place to another. Living out our daily lives as if the things that happen to us are the most important thing in the whole world.

That is when we are reminded again that we are not in control.
That you are the one who numbers our days and sustains our lives.

We pray that we will be serious about life.
that we will be kind and gentle to those we love,
that we will care for those we are responsible for,
and we pray for enough grace to love some who are unlovable.

Help us to realize that you did not come into this world to minister to the good people. Remind us that you loved those that no one else would love.

We can not follow your example without an outpouring of your grace.
Help us to depend on the power that only you can give.

FINAL PEACE

As we get older
We become more and more aware
That death is inevitable.

Somehow when death
Is not a threat
But is a reality,
We begin to understand
The anguish of Christ
In the garden of Gethsemane.

It takes a few years
And some grey hair
And at times the gross impact of tragedy
To know what Luke meant when he said,
"Sweat like great drops of blood."

We know about death.
We see is all around us.
We see it in all of its finality.

All things die—
From cells to stars.

It is the resurrection
That is illogical.

We pray for resurrection—
We talk about eternal life—
We sing about, "The home over there,"
But why do we have to die
To achieve it?

Why all the pain?
The suffering?
The agony?
Why is death such a struggle?

Why can't we find the peace
That Jesus found
In the garden of Gethsemane
When He prayed
"Not my will but Thine be done?"

Is it that final peace cannot be found
Until final peace is needed?

Bear with us Father.
We may be kicking, screaming
And fighting our way through life
But in due time
We will come home—
We will make peace—
When it is necessary to make peace!

FAITH

When the answer to our
most heartfelt prayers
is a resounding no,
faith may be shaken
but it is never destroyed.

Faith that is never tested
can never grow.

It is only when we reach the
limit of our understanding
that faith becomes operative.

Until then we operate on knowledge,
but knowledge can never
solve the mysteries of life.

Faith can not solve
the mysteries,
but with faith there is no need
to solve mysteries.

Faith makes life
within the mysteries,
rich and rewarding.

TO LOVE THE UNLOVELY

"but love your enemies, and do good, and lend, hoping for nothing gain; and your reward will be great, . . ."

Luke 6:35

Remind us that your commandment to love is not contingent on

> Happiness
> Success
> Approval
> Contentment
> Joy
> Peace

Remind us that your commandment that we love one another does not depend on

> Agreement
> Harmony
> Understanding
> Conformity
> Togetherness
> Reciprocity

Remind us that the absence of love does not release us from the obligation to love even though we are

> Hurt
> Lonely
> Angry

Disappointed
Afraid
Threatened

Remind us that the primary expression of your love was death
on the cross

Betrayed
Abused
Tortured
Exposed
Rejected
Forsaken

Otherwise we have no hope of obeying your commandment
that we love our enemies.

SPONTANEOUS LOVE

When we were little children huddled around our mother's knees we were taught that, "It is more blessed to give than to receive."

And during the years of our impressionable youth we came to know the lonely Galilean who taught us that the giving of one's self in love is the will of God for every person.

And in our mature years we have felt the quickening of the Holy Spirit which enabled us to love some who otherwise would have been unlovable and were thereby taught that the love of God really does flow through us.

Then why do we have this insatiable hunger to be loved? Why does every fiber of our bodies ache to be caressed, to be soothed, to be loved? Why do we reach out like drowning men for mere twigs of compassion and tenderness?

Does the giving of love create this intense need to be loved? When we love enough to expose the raw places of our souls why does it hurt so much? Must we be whip sawed between the need to love and the need to be loved?

And then, thank God, when we least expect it—it happens! A spontaneous outburst of mutual, joyous love, the ecstasy of which sustains us as we do the work of love in your kingdom.

HEALING

When the message was sent
That yet another operation was necessary
My sister sent the following reply.

"My heart aches and my love is with you.
I will come, if only to hold your hand
And drain a portion of your pain into my body."

I have always heard of healing
By the laying on of hands
But until now I did not understand!

Thank you Lord for hands
That are connected to hearts
That have the capacity to absorb pain.

DADDY'S LITTLE FINGER

Sometimes when we begin to pray,
And say. "Our Father which art in heaven,"
Our thoughts go back to when we were little children.

We remember how we would
Hold on to daddy's little finger
And how that finger
Was all the security we could ever ask for,
And although we are now grown
We still hunger for that same sense of security.

> Oh, Heavenly Father help us to trust in you
> With the same simple trust
> That long ago we placed in daddy's little finger.

We remember that when we went away
To that far off land called first grade,
Or to that strange place called college,
Or to that frightful country called war,
Our fathers would embrace us
And tell us that they loved us
And that nothing could ever take away that love,
Regardless of where we might go,
Regardless of what might happen.

> Oh, Heavenly Father embrace us just now
> And reassure us that you love us,
> Regardless of where we might go,
> Regardless of what might happen.

We remember that our fathers would teach us
By showing us how to chop wood,

Or how to drive the car,
Or how to face life's ambiguities,
And we would watch him
With the intensity that can belong only to a child
And then try to imitate his very mannerisms,
And when we failed he would teach us again
With tenderness and patience.

> Oh, Heavenly Father teach us just now
> By giving us the vision of Jesus dying on the cross,
> Showing us how to face insecurity,
> How to live with rejection,
> How to accept injustice.
>
> Help us to imitate the example of Jesus,
> Give us the courage to give our lives away
> And to die if necessary for others.

GREY DAYS

Jesus,
You knew about mountain tops and
You knew about the depths of despair,
But we wonder if You knew about grey days
Filled with fog?

It is days filled with grey shapeless fog
That give us problems.
We get so busy finding our way through the fog
That we lose things;
> Friends,
> Marriages,
> Children,
> Health,
> Jobs,
> Hope.

When You came to seek and to save
That which was lost
Did You also look for all those things
We lose in the fog of day by day living?

Jesus,
Please come with your tender hand
And lead us out of these foggy days
Into the sunshine of Your presence.

Grant us,
Just enough guidance to find our way through the fog,
Just enough grace to end this day in peace, and
Just enough joy to be able to look forward to tomorrow.

REFLECTIONS ON SCRIPTURE

AWESOME

"I have called you friends".

John 15:15

When Jesus said to his disciples,
"I have called you friends"
He made one of the most awesome statements ever made.

We think of Jesus as:
    Lord,
    Savior,
    God
And sometimes even as Judge
But he called his disciples friends!

The emotion conveyed by the word friend is profound.
It says:
    Companion,
    Caregiver,
    Confidant
And in John 15 it says co-worker.

Now that is awesome!
Jesus is our friend
And our co-worker.

"What a friend we have in Jesus!"

REJOICE!

"Now the God of hope fill you with all joy and peace in believing,
That ye may abound in hope through the power of the Holy Ghost."

Romans 15:13

You cannot change what happened yesterday,
But you can change your attitude today.

Do not look at what you lost.
Look at what you have left.

Rejoice while you are waiting.
You can live in hope today.

Live in expectation of what God has in store for you.
Be patient while you wait.

Rejoice as if it is already done.

GETTING OUT OF THE BOAT

"And Peter said, Lord if it be thou, bid me come. And he said, "Come."

Matthew 14: 28 and 29

It was not all that comfortable in the boat but it was not as scary as being in the water.

Most of us are willing to serve as long as we can stay in the boat.

There are two questions,
"Are you willing to get out of the boat?" and
"Are your eyes fixed upon Jesus?"

They were doing what they had been told to do.
They never expected to see Jesus in the midst of the sea.
But when the master said, "Come."
Peter got out of the boat!

The Lord put you in the boat and the Lord can call you out of the boat!
And remember, even if you take your eyes off the master and begin to sink salvation is only a word away.

When the Master says, "Come"
Get out of the boat!

And keep your eyes upon Jesus!

BUT!

"But we are all as an unclean thing and all our righteousness are as filthy rags; . . . . But, now O Lord, thou art our Father; we are the clay and thou our potter and we are the work of thy hand.

Isaiah 64:6 and 8

God has hidden his face from us.
We deserve the withdrawal of his blessings.

But!

He is our Father.
He is our loving Father.
He is our forgiving Father.

And Jesus said,
    "His father saw him,
    and had compassion,
    and RAN,
    and fell on his neck,
    and kissed him."

Remember,

God is waiting,
God has been waiting all along,
God has been waiting with complete forgiveness.

And he is not only waiting,

God is seeking,
God is wooing,
God is pursuing

With arms wide open,
he is running toward us,
Even now!

Praise his name.

ALMS

"But when thou doest alms, let not thy left hand knoweth what thy right hand doeth."

Matthew 6:4

What are your motives? Remember that religion can be unhealthy. It can even be ungodly.

Mark Twain had a famous saying, "A good man in the worse sense of the word".

True Christianity is the exact opposite of much of today' popular culture.
"If you got it, flaunt it!"

Dr. James Hatley told a story about a group of Nuns who went to live in the slums of Paris.

They left their habits behind.
They told no one who they were.
They did not evangelize.
They did not claim to be Christians.
They did good where they found need.
They loved everyone they met.

Later the people came to them and asked, "Why are you different?"
Then they told them.

Giving alms is directed toward others.
Prayer is directed toward God.
Fasting is directed toward self.

My grandmother Smith would get so burdened about someone in the community who was under conviction she could not eat. She would lose weight until the person was saved. My grandfather would say, "Lou Vinnie, You're go'in to dry up and blow away if that boy don't hurry up and get saved."

Why do we give?
Why do we pray?
Why or perhaps I should say do we ever fast?

HEALED BUT NOT WHOLE

*"Were there not ten cleansed? . . . And he said to him, . . . thy
faith hath made thee whole."*

Luke 17:17-19

Jesus did not tell them to come back.
They had no obligation to come back.
The nine who did not come back did not loose their healing.
The Samaritan came back on his own.
He came back because he was greatful.

He had a deeper understanding of the love of God.
He had a deeper appreciation of the mercy of God.

Remember the ten asked for mercy,
Not for healing!
They all received healing,

But in a sense the Samaritan was the only one who received
mercy!

" . . . he said to him . . . thy faith hath made thee whole."

The nine were healed but they were not made whole!

God grant that we will be grateful,
We want to be more than healed.
We want to be whole!

BE PREPARED!

"Prepare ye the way of the Lord, make his paths straight."

"Every valley shall be filled, and every mountain and hill shall be brought low; and the crooked shall be made straight, and the rough ways shall be made smooth;"

Luke 3:4&5

John the Baptist was preaching in the wilderness, announcing the coming of the Messiah.

It is interesting that these sentences are a specification for road building. Road building is hard work. Even with the advantage of large earthmoving machines and modern explosives it is still hard work. When John spoke these words it was even harder work.

When the king came to visit, an army of men went ahead to repair the roads and rebuild the bridges and make the rough ways smooth.

The Messiah, the spiritual king, is coming. Repent and get your spiritual road ready for the king.

Are we willing to prepare the way for the Lord?

Are we able to make our rough lives smooth?

Are we up to the task of clearing out the briars and brambles?

Can we find the repentance necessary for the remission of sins?

Can we bear to level out the rough places?

Can we get ready for the Messiah?

Be Prepared!

WATCH OUT

"And he was teaching in one of the synagogues on the Sabbath and behold there was a woman which has a spirit of infirmity for eighteen years . . . . and he laid his hands on her: and immediately she was made straight . . ."

Luke 13: 10, 11 and 13

Watch out!

Jesus is coming!

He is causing trouble.

He is breaking the rules.

He is determined to love.

He will not let anything get in the way.

Watch out!

Watch him love!

"Jesus Loves Me this I Know".

I WISH I HAD A MARY TO LISTEN TO ME

" . . . she had a sister called Mary, which also sat at Jesus' feet, and heard his word.

Luke 10:39

Jesus, during those last few troublesome days
When you were facing rejection,
When the tentacles of death were reaching out to ensnare you,
Mary was there.

She did not make suggestions.
She gave no advice.
She offered no solutions.
She did not change anything.
But she was there,
She cared,
She listened.

You have given me a Martha who is the joy of my life.
She loves me with such devotion
I am convinced
That she would not hesitate for one second
To lay down her life for me.

So, you see Jesus,
I love her so much
I cannot compound her fear
By exposing mine.

To talk of my anxiety
Would only heighten hers.
I instinctively protect her at all cost.
I am always careful
To tremble with my body rigid.

Jesus, you had a Mary
Who simply wanted to sit at your feet
And listen to you.
If you know of another Mary
Who would like to listen to me,
Would you please tell her that I need her?

CONFESSION

" . . . blind Bartimaeus, sat by the highway begging. He began
to cry out . . . Jesus thou son of David, have mercy on me."

Mark 10:46 and 47

Prayer is the confession of truth to God.
Prayer is the out flowing of our lives to God.
Prayer is the confession of our needs to God.

It is not what we desire,
It is what we need to make our lives right
That makes prayer so important.

To love God regardless.
To love God because we cannot help ourselves.
To love god because we can do nothing else.

The result does not matter.
It is the confession that matters.

Honesty between man and God is the essence of reality.

A STAFF

"And the Lord said unto him, What is that in thine hand?
And he said, A staff. And he said, Cast it on the ground".

Exodus 4:2-3

What is that in your hand Moses?
    A staff.
Throw it on the ground.
    It became a snake.
Pick it up Moses.
    It became a staff.

When he threw it on the ground, it became "God's staff".
It had always been God's staff but Moses did not know it.
He thought it was his staff.
It did not have power until it became "God's staff".

Use what you have.
Throw your staff on the ground.
Do what you can.
See what God can do.

AUTHOR BIOGRAPHY

Andrew Smith graduated from high school in 1950 and then joined the US Navy in 1951. He then started his study in architecture at Georgia Institute of Technology and received his Barch in 1960.

While he was in college he served as the pastor of a small rural church just north of Atlanta called Dunwoody Baptist. His four years as a pastor were in many ways successful and he led the congregation to make important and far reaching decisions.

Contrary to the expectations of the day he did not feel a call to the professional ministry and began his career in architecture in 1961. In the ensuing 51 years he has designed many types of buildings in over 20 states. He now serves as an Associate Principal in Self Tucker Architects in Memphis Tennessee.

He has been married to Mary Jo Mynatt for 59 years. They have been members of Second Baptist Church in Memphis for 45 years where he has served in many ways. They have a daughter, two sons and three grandchildren.

CPSIA information can be obtained at www.ICGtesting.com
Printed in the USA
LVOW082241240412

278976LV00002B/1/P